Rethinking Dry Eye Treatment

Lifestyle changes to control dry eye

Written by Dr. Travis Zigler,

Edited by Dr. Jenna Zigler

<u>Join the Dry Eye Syndrome Support Community on Facebook</u>

Presented by:

Use the code DRYEYE20 to get 20% off your first Heyedrate order on <u>Amazon</u>

<u>**Click here to shop: http://amzn.to/2xvBA7u**</u>

<u>www.dryeyecommunity.com</u>

TABLE OF CONTENTS

Chapter 1 - Introduction to the Power of Food

Before we dive into this journey on food, I want to talk to all of you about the struggle of dry eye disease and disease in general. Regardless of where you are in this dry eye adventure, know that from this moment forward, you have a choice - you can choose whether you want to feel amazing or just get by. Take this opportunity to set the bar for how you want to live the rest of your life...feeling great or feeling lousy. The choice is YOURS. I promise that if you follow the steps laid out in the upcoming chapters, you will be feeling more incredible than you ever thought possible.

The next few chapters are from my deep dive into books, holistic medicine, nutrition and also talking to leading experts in these fields. I had given myself two days to write the section on food helping your dry eye and here I sit almost two months later still trying to format it correctly. I am even considering breaking this off and creating a whole book around food itself. It's that important! Enjoy this new opportunity to take back your life and TAKE ACTION to feel happier with yourself and feel more confident than ever before.

"Nature knows when you are in harmony with yourself and your environment... We frantically go to a doctor to see if they can fix [my problems]. They can't; only YOU can." --Dr. Randine Lewis, PhD

The Word Diet

I use the term diet in this book a lot. I do not believe in dieting and the word diet is used to describe what we will be eating. You are not going on a diet. You are starting a new diet of healthy foods that will completely transform your life and if you stick to this diet, you can eat as much as you want inside of it. Again, you are not going on a diet, but rather changing what you eat.

What is Disease?

The most commonly cited causes of disease are lack of oxygen, inflammation, hormonal imbalance, and microorganisms (bacteria, viruses, etc...). There are numerous culprits that can lead to any of these four causes and they can include: animal fats, dairy, sugar, and toxic chemicals. These foods can increase estrogen levels, flood the body with toxic chemicals, and carry life threatening bacteria. We will explore each section in much more detail later.

What you put in your mouth is one of the biggest factors affecting how your body works and feels. The cleaner, more oxygen-pumping, anti-inflammatory, hormone balancing, and nutrient filled food you put in your body, the better your body can do what you ask of it.

Katherine Thurer, MD says

"Diet is HUGE! It has an enormous role in every aspect of our health across the board. Switching to an anti-inflammatory diet is the number one thing I recommend."

So Where Are The Studies?

There is not much scientific evidence on diet and disease, because there is not a lot of money in it. Pharmaceutical companies have billions of dollars to sponsor international studies about their medications to get them approved for a disease symptom. Farmers that grow organic crops don't have this same financial luxury.

The unfortunate realization is that Western medicine (which is only one way of treatment) is this:

1. Patient has problem that needs to be addressed, so they head to their doctor.
2. Doctor has sales representatives from various companies come in all day, everyday explaining to them why their drug is better.
3. Doctor then uses the newest medication to treat the SYMPTOM of the patient's problem.
4. If that treatment doesn't take, the doctor switches to another medication that another company claims will work.
5. Then, if that treatment doesn't work, doctors have to resort to surgery to fix the problem.

We were taught this method of medicine. We believed in this method of medicine. Until we questioned it...

Our Shifting Belief from Western Medicine to Eastern Medicine

It was early 2015, and we had just moved to South Carolina, from Ohio, to start our two new optometry practices! I promised my wife that after we moved, we could start trying for children. So we did...

Five months into trying to have children, we realized that it was not as easy as all our friends said it was. We started exploring what could be causing this problem. I was tested to make sure I was fertile, but that wasn't the problem. Jenna was tested and found that she had polycystic ovaries.

Numerous lab tests were run, but aside from polycystic ovaries shown on ultrasound, hormone levels and nutrient levels were all normal. Because it appeared Jenna was "healthy", we were diagnosed with unexplained infertility complicated by polycystic ovaries... the most frustrating of all diagnoses in those trying to get pregnant! We began with a few monthly rounds of Clomid and metformin, which all failed to achieve the desired result. We were then prescribed Letrozole, in hopes that it would work in a different way. It didn't. Through these pharmaceutical interventions come a lot of undesired side effects including sleeplessness, anxiety, mood swings, rage, thirst, and more.

Finally in July of 2016, we were told by our fertility doctor that we would have to do IVF (In Vitro Fertilization), which costs anywhere from $10,000 to $25,000 with a 33% chance of success. Not to mention the massive amount of expensive pharmaceuticals and chemicals that Jenna would have to put in her body in order to possibly conceive. This is not including the emotional toll of IVF on both the woman trying to conceive and the husband as well. With that being said, there is a place for IVF, we just didn't think it was for us.

The night before our first IVF appointment while lying in bed, I turned to Jenna and told her that I didn't believe that IVF was right for us. I expressed that there had to be a better way, and she agreed. This led us on a journey to explore additional routes of medicine including Eastern medicine, which is about finding out what is causing this distress in your body and healing it from the inside out.

We were already eating a plant-based diet, with minimal meat consumption of about one time per month. We then switched to eating only organic food.

At the recommendation of a few friends, Jenna started receiving weekly acupuncture treatments. Her acupuncturist started her on a healthy, high fat diet (more on this later) and reduced the amount of carbs and sugar she was consuming. Four more months passed and still no results, although her progress with acupuncture looked promising.

In February, our acupuncturist told us that her temperature chart that month looked perfect, and that we may conceive the next weekend. In the meantime, losing hope after two and a half years of trying, we scheduled an adoption meeting to begin the process.

The day before the adoption meeting, we took a pregnancy test... It was positive.

And here I am writing this section of our book one month before Baby Z is born (I convinced Jenna to not find out the sex).

This shifted my belief in how I practiced medicine as an eye doctor. I started thinking that maybe every time I prescribe a medication I am just covering up a symptom to a much larger problem going on with the body. I started exploring different methods of healing disease from the inside out. Which leads me to present day and writing this book for you.

Please know that the methods I discuss in this book are NOT just for dry eye, but for healing the entire body of ailments such as high blood pressure, diabetes, cholesterol, arthritis, infertility, and any other symptoms you have.

Chapter 2 - Embracing Foods That Heal

Food can be the ultimate source of healing or the ultimate destruction of your body. Once you clear away the junk that's clogging your body from years of poor diet (by the way, it's not your fault... it's the government, big pharma, and factory farms), you will unclog your mind as well. You'll be able to tap into your healthiest and happiest you.

All of this starts with plants!

A healthy, plant-based diet is the consumption of nutrient-dense plant foods while minimizing processed foods, oils, and animal foods (including dairy products and eggs). It encourages lots of vegetables (cooked or raw), fruits, beans, peas, lentils, soybeans, seeds, and nuts.

Plants help balance our hormones, maintain a stable blood sugar and pressure, and generally fuel all of our systems in a cleaner, more efficient way. Plant-based foods are nature's way of giving us sun-powered health at its most delicious. There are virtually no nutrients in animal-based foods - including protein and iron - that aren't better provided by plants. They can supercharge your body, reduce diseases like cancer, heart disease, diabetes, osteoporosis, and help you live the life you've always dreamed of.

Research done by Drs. T Colin Campbell, Caldwell B Esselstyn Jr., and John McDougall have shown that changing diet to include more plant based foods and less animal-based foods can help you live longer, feel younger, lose weight, have more energy, preserve your eyesight, keep your mind sharp, and have a more vibrant sex life. They also discuss that it can eliminate your need for pharmaceutical drugs, especially for treating things like depression, type 2 diabetes, and high blood pressure.

Fiber

Fiber is at the top of the list of health benefits of plants. Fiber helps "scrub" our intestines clean of all the junk that inhabits them on a daily basis. Since we don't digest fiber, it helps move things along from entrance to exit, but also absorbs chemicals and toxins along the way out. A lack of fiber can cause constipation, bloating, hemorrhoids, gas, and diseases like intestinal or colon cancer.

The more fiber you eat the lower your risk for diabetes, high blood pressure, high cholesterol, and rectal and colon cancer.

Phytochemicals

Phytochemicals, such as carotenoids, act like shields that soak up invaders and keep them from harming the plants' tissues. Our bodies cannot fight against these free radicals, industrial pollutants, or toxins hiding in animal foods. These cause our bodies and tissues to start breaking down, which can lead to Alzheimer's, dementia, cataracts, hardening of the arteries, cancer, emphysema, and arthritis. If we eat plants, they lend us their powers to fight these toxins. Each plant has its own fighting ability, which is why a variety of plants is key to your diet.

A side bonus of phytochemicals is that they help with wrinkles by protecting your skin from damage and helping your skin produce more collagen. Whole grains are packed with B-complex vitamins which help with glowing skin.

Carotenoids are responsible for giving fruits and vegetables like carrots, tomatoes, and bell peppers their bright orange, yellow, and red hues. A few types of carotenoids, including zeaxanthin, lutein, and beta carotene, play a critical role in maintaining eye health. They benefit our eyes by guarding against vision loss, while improving one's ability to see colors and fine detail. Additionally they also play a role in protecting our eyes against damaging effects of UV light we encounter outdoors as well as blue light from our computers, phones, tablets, and TVs.

Susan Levin, MD, RD, staff dietician with the Physicians Committee for Responsible Medicine says

"Women who follow vegan diets are often healthier than [those] who consume meat, thanks to eating lower levels of saturated fats (BAD omega-6's, more on this later) and cholesterol and higher levels of fiber, folate, and cancer-fighting antioxidants and phytochemicals."

Let's dive into inflammation and what it causes.

Chapter 3 - Chronic (Long-Standing) Inflammation

Inflammation is a BIG deal. Most disease is some form of inflammation, so battling inflammation is a key component to battling your dry eye and other eye diseases. An estimated 80% of visits to doctor's offices are for issues relating to a chronic disease, which stems from chronic inflammation of the body. The CDC states that 7 out of every 10 Americans die of chronic disease.

According to Dr. Mercola in the article How Inflammation Affects Every Aspect of Your Health,

"The presence of inflammation is what makes most disease perceptible to an individual. It can and often does occur for years before it exists at levels sufficient to be apparent or clinically significant... One could also argue that without inflammation most disease would not even exist.... The fact that your immune system drives the inflammatory process in disease is well established. Unfortunately Western medicine offers little in the way of actual answers as to managing or overcoming the Autoimmune process... The typical approach to therapy is generally to suppress the immune response with Immune suppressive agents or sometimes steroids (Restasis and Xiidra perform this way for dry eye). Both approaches are designed to reduce inflammation but neither stops the underlying disease processes or allows for damaged tissues to regenerate... Unless you turn OFF the actual cause of fire (inflammation), all you have done is postponed the inevitable and potentially destroyed more of the building (your body) in the process, by allowing the fire (inflammation) to smolder in a subclinical fashion."

Let's also look at the DEWS II (The Tear Film and Ocular Surface Society's Dry Eye Workshop in 2017) definition of dry eye, in which it states that inflammation is one of the key reasons for dry eye.

*"Dry eye is a multifactorial disease of the ocular surface characterized by a loss of homeostasis of the tear film, and accompanied by ocular symptoms, in which tear film instability and hyperosmolarity, **ocular surface inflammation and damage**, and neurosensory abnormalities play etiological roles,"*

Short Term Effects of Inflammation on the Body

- Dry Eye
- Headache
- Fatigue – feeling tired
- Dilated pupils
- Stiff neck and shoulder pain

- Back pain
- Increased heart rate
- Sweaty palms and feet
- Upset stomach
- Depression

Long Term Effects of Inflammation on the Body

Meat is loaded with saturated fat, which contributes to the following chronic conditions:

- Dry Eye
- High Blood Pressure
- Type 2 Diabetes
- High Cholesterol
- Heart Attacks
- Strokes
- Heart Disease
- Alzheimer's
- Thyroid Disease
- Arthritis
- Cancer
- Allergies
- Psoriasis and Eczema
- Osteoporosis
- Digestive conditions such as colitis and diverticulitis

Chapter 4 - How Do We Reduce Inflammation?

#1 Way To Reduce Inflammation: Plant-Based Alkalizing Diet

Katherine Thurer, MD explains "Diet is HUGE! It has an enormous role in every aspect of our health across the board. Switching to an anti-inflammatory diet is the number one thing I recommend."

The quote above sums up the importance of eating to combat inflammation. Plants have an incredible alkalizing effect on the body, which fights inflammation. A diet high in whole plant foods can help rebalance the body's estrogen levels since all that fiber helps rid the body of excess substances it doesn't need, including detoxified hormones. Plant-based diets can also reverse obesity, which is linked to diabetes and high blood pressure.

But I Can't Live Without Meat!! - MYTH

Before we dive into what to eat, please take note. If you have not eaten like this before your body has adapted to eating meat, dairy, and processed food. Much like a long term smoker goes through a detoxification, you will also go through a detoxification in which your body may develop rashes, headaches, shakes, phlegm, sleeplessness, constipation, diarrhea, or other forms of discomfort. YOU WILL GET THROUGH THIS.

Don't get overwhelmed with the lists of foods to eat. We have included a simple meal preparation chart further along.

Let's dive into what to eat.

Vegetables

I bet you didn't see this one coming. A plant-based alkalizing diet's staple is… PLANTS! Sounds boring right? WRONG! Plants are one of the most exciting things on this earth. Make sure to get plenty of variety with vegetables, as colors are your friends to get those phytochemicals we discussed earlier.

Instead of thinking of vegetables as sides, they need to be your main dish. When picking vegetables to eat, focus on leafy green vegetables taking up most of your plate. The healthiest options are organic frozen vegetables then organic fresh vegetables. Frozen is healthier due to the fact it is flash frozen right after being picked and doesn't have time to lose nutrients on the way to you.

What vegetables to eat (not an exhaustive list: Spinach, Kale, Mustard Greens, Watercress, Hearts of Romaine, Raw Broccoli, Bok Choy, Swiss Chard, Collards, Dandelion, Boston Lettuce, Cabbage, Cauliflower, Peas, Carrots, Peppers, Celery, Corn, Tomato, Asparagus, Green Beans, Cucumber, Zucchini, Squash, Sweet Potatoes.

Super-Powered Vegetables/Foods

Experiment, experiment, experiment with these exotic foods to add an extra super-power punch to your dishes. These include unemboshi plums, miso, parsnips, rutabaga, burdock root, daikon, lotus root, fermented vegetables, and sea vegetables. Green leafy vegetables are included in super-powered foods and are included in the above list.

Sea Vegetables

Don't be intimidated by the weird names. Sea vegetables are filled with vitamins and minerals and include nori, hijiki, arame, wakame, and kombu. They are also high in protein, help alkalize the blood, are a great detoxifying agent, reduce blood pressure, and inhibit cancerous growths.

Fermented/Pickled Vegetables

Fermented veggies contain probiotics which are great for healing the gut (stomach, intestines, and colon). Probiotics help your body absorb nutrients, boost your immune system, and are great antioxidants.

Pickled vegetables include pickles, sauerkraut, and kimchi. However DON'T buy these in the grocery aisle as they are full of preservatives, but instead look in the refrigerator section for unpasteurized products, which will contain many more probiotics and be better for you.

These can be added to any meal to add a little bit of flavor, tang, crunch, or salt.

Grains

Whole grains are considered one of the best forms of energy that we can eat. Believe it or not, these little gems are packed with protein, fiber, and other good for you nutrients. They help us break down protein, cleanse and detoxify our system, protect our cells, release energy, and keep our hearts healthy. They are also rich in B-complex vitamins.

Grains to eat include quinoa, millet, spelt, brown rice, wild rice, farro, barley, oats, and bulgur. Mix these up so you are not consuming the same grains every week. Start with quick cooking grains first to allow for easier digestion then move to the regular ones as your body adjusts.

Beans

Beans, beans, the magical fruit... Literally, these things are magic. There are a variety of ways to eat beans as well, such as in hummus, tacos, burritos, soup, chili, and more.

Beans to eat include navy beans, black beans, chickpeas, cannellini beans, red kidney beans, lentils, tofu, and edamame.

Fruits

Fruit does wonders for your body and contains vitamins, minerals, phytochemicals, and fiber. It can help protect against cardiovascular disease, diabetes, and cancer, but must be consumed in moderation. Also, avoid juices which do not contain the fiber of the fruit therefore just giving you a heavy dose of sugar. When eating whole fruit try to limit this to two to three cups daily.

ORGANIC fruits to add to your diet include strawberries, blueberries, blackberries, raspberries, mango

banana, no-sugar-added pitted dates, no-sugar-added apricots, no-sugar-added raisins, grapes, apples, oranges, melon, pineapple, kiwi, peaches, plums, papaya, pear, and coconut.

#2 Way To Reduce Inflammation: AVOID these foods

Filling your diet with foods that are nutritionally deficient and have high saturated fats is the quickest way to derail the balance of your body. If your body is busy fighting the damage caused from foods like ice cream, hamburgers, and pepperoni pizza after mealtimes, then you will lack energy, feel depressed, and want to sleep due to all energy being exerted to the meal you just had.

DON'T WORRY, though. If you've eaten terribly your whole life, it is not too late. Choose to turn the switch now to a healthier lifestyle and accept the challenges that come with it. Start eating healthy today and your body will heal your past wrong doings, because of its incredible ability to heal.

This will be a tough challenge, so I always recommend a cheat day. This is 12 hours in which you can eat anything and everything you have been craving that whole week. Make it count, but then go back to the healthy, feel better foods for the other 156 hours in a week.

Try this out for a test... For a full day make a green smoothie for breakfast, lunch, and dinner. Write down the answers to the following questions:

Did I feel tired all day?

Did I feel like I needed an afternoon nap?

Was I unmotivated to do my most important work at my job?

Did I poop?

Was I bloated?

Did I feel like drinking more caffeine to stay awake?

Did I experience cramping?

How did I feel the day after I ate all this?

Now eat eggs, bacon, and toast for breakfast, a hamburger and fries for lunch, and a chicken breast with potatoes for dinner. Answer the same questions above.

So, What Foods Should I Avoid?

You have been eating the wrong foods for almost your whole life. However it is NOT your fault. It is the government, factory farms, and large companies that are to blame. These are the people that told you "Eat meat for strength," "The other white meat," "Drink milk for healthy bones," "Got Milk?" and "Eat fortified bread and cereal for your vitamins."

Meat, dairy, and processed foods like cereal and bread are toxic to your body. They're clogging your arteries, raising your blood pressure, and pumping you full of cholesterol, toxins, hormones, and antibiotics that you don't need. According to the World Health Organization (WHO), a diet high in animal products such as meat, dairy, and eggs, as well as high in sugar-laden and fat-laden processed foods such as breads, cereals, chips, cakes, and cookies, cause an increase in the acidity of your body, which causes bodywide inflammation. Diets that are heavy in these sources (animal products and processed foods) cause 80% of cardiovascular disease, more than 33% of all cancers, and virtually all obesity and type 2 diabetes in this country.

Heart disease, for example, is the number one killer of women in the United States and is linked to high amounts of saturated fat in animal products. But it doesn't just clog up your arteries around your heart (heart disease). It clogs up ALL your arteries, leading to strokes, cancer, and tissue death due to lack of oxygen.

First Food To Avoid: Meat

Meat carries numerous hormones, antibiotics, pesticides, pollutants, bacteria, and viruses into your body. We store all this in our body fat, so it continues to fester inside our body even after it's been digested. When you stop eating meat, you stop eating extra hormones, prevent antibiotic overdose, avoid toxic pesticides, eliminate dangerous pollutants, and decrease exposure to scary viruses and bacteria.

The FDA and USDA allow factory farmers to use hormones to promote growth and milk production in their cattle. Two out of every three cattle raised for slaughter are treated with natural and synthetic forms of estrogen and progesterone and other hormones linked to breast cancer and colon cancer in humans. These hormones cause a slew of problems and affect the entire food chain as they get passed on to humans that consume the animal product, the surrounding ecosystem including plants and fish soak up the hormones as well causing an imbalance in humans.

Due to the crowded nature of factory farms, livestock is literally standing in feet of its own fecal matter which is filled with bacteria and can cause widespread illness among the livestock. To combat this, factory farmers mix low dose antibiotics into the feed and water. 80% of all antibiotics in the US are sold to farmers for this purpose. Massive resistance to these antibiotics is a huge problem that could potentially extinct the human population (words for a different book). These are given to all livestock to prevent disease in these crowded and unsanitary conditions.

Factory farmers use toxic pesticides to ward off insects, kill weeds, and protect their financial investment. This is the same feed that is mixed with antibiotics and hormones to feed the livestock. We can usually wash most of this off our produce or not use it at all with organic produce, but animals absorb the pesticides in the food they eat, which ends up in your dinner.

Persistent organic pollutants (POPs) are environment chemicals from industrial processes, pharmaceuticals, and pesticides that have soaked in the water supply and soil. These POPs accumulate and continue moving up the food chain to you. 89% of our POP intake comes from meat sources and dairy, including eggs and fish. Some POPs like dioxins, are Group 1 carcinogens, and cling to animal fats. Even low level exposure has been shown to increase the incidence of infertility, diabetes, learning disabilities, immune system suppression, and lung problems.

Finally, according to the USDA, 70% of foodborne illness in the US is from meat that is contaminated with bacteria like E.coli, listeria, and campylobacter. This is most likely due to these animals being fed food that is not meant to be digested in their intestines (grain versus grass). Due to poor slaughtering practices, intestinal contents (poop) splash across meat and contaminate it.

Aren't you excited for the cocktail of hormones, antibiotics, pesticides, pollutants, and bacteria that are on the plate of beef, chicken or pork waiting for your consumption?

What About Fish?

Most fish have become too toxic to consume. Oceans are slowly becoming so polluted with garbage that fish are beginning to eat our garbage as part of their diet and it is showing up further up the food line when we consume the fish. Fish also contain high levels of mercury, organochlorines, polychlorinated biphenyls (PCBs) and other toxins that can wreak havoc on your body.

Omega-3 fatty acids are good at lowering the risk of heart disease, improving blood vessel function, and improving overall health of people with diabetes, cholesterol, and other diseases. However we can also get these health benefits from vegan omega-3-rich sources like walnuts, chia, hemp, and flaxseeds.

What About Eggs?

Eggs contain lutein, omega-3, and protein. They are an extremely viable source of all three, but there are plant-based substitutes that are even better like those listed above.

My final thoughts on meat. If you still, after reading that, want to eat meat or have to have it, consider only eating organic, free-range, and local meat where you know where it is coming from. Do we still eat meat? Yes, about once a month. If you feel like you have to eat it daily, limit it to dinner only.

I will challenge you to try a meatless week and see how you feel. Later on we will discuss different ideas for breakfast, lunch, snacks, and dinner.

Foods to eliminate = meat

- Beef
- Chicken
- Pork
- Fish
- Eggs

Second Food to Avoid: Dairy

Like meat, dairy contains growth hormones and antibiotics due to animal treatment explained above. Dairy has also been shown to cause inflammation which leads to life-threatening illness like MS, type 1 diabetes, rheumatoid arthritis, and hyperthyroidism.

Consider that humans are the only animals on the planet that consume another species' milk. Cow's milk is a fairly recent addition to our diets. Milk protein is hard for humans to digest, if they can digest it at all, which triggers an autoimmune attack and inflammation in the body.

Dairy products are also our biggest sources of saturated fats and sugar. Lactose, which is the sugar in milk, contributes the same calorie load as soda ounce for ounce according to Neal Barnard, president of the Physicians Committee for Responsible Medicine.

Foods to Eliminate	Replace with
Milk	Almond Milk, Cashew Milk
Cheese	Nutritional Yeast
Yogurt	Coconut Yogurt (plain)
Cottage Cheese, Ricotta Cheese	Coconut Yogurt (plain)
Sour Cream	Coconut Yogurt (plain)

Third Food to Avoid: Sugar

Sugar causes inflammation, makes you overweight, leads to diabetes, and is linked to cancer. How do you feel after consuming that sugary cookie, cake, or donut? I feel like garbage and I'm sure you do too. Headaches, mood swings, depression, and more are symptoms of sugar intake.

Don't worry though, nature makes its own sweets. I challenge you to throw away all the white, brown, and powdered sugar in your cabinet, along with all the foods that contain these harmful granules. After that do not eat anything with added sugar for a week. If you get a craving, reach for a nice bowl of ripe berries or frozen grapes, or better yet, make some banana ice cream.

Refined sugar - along with dextrose, maltose, evaporated cane juice, high-fructose corn syrup, and agave - can take your body on a blood sugar roller coaster, which sends your pancreas into a insulin producing craze, which increases your risk significantly for diabetes. Type 2 diabetes is when your insulin production cannot keep up with the sugar load and your pancreas may stop working. This sugar roller coaster will also cause depression, mood swings, and craving for more sugar creating a never ending cycle.

Artificial Sweeteners are chemical products made in a lab that have no long term studies on the effects on the human body. Avoid these at all costs. This includes NutraSweet, Equal, Sweet 'N Low, Splenda, and Stevia.

Foods to Eliminate	Replace with
Pop or Soda (diet and regular)	Flavored Sparkling Water Water with lemon, lime squeezed in Water diffused with cucumber, mint
Sugar-filled coffee beverages (lattes, mochas, cappuccino)	Organic Black Coffee (decaf or regular)
Cookies, cakes, pies, and brownies	Organic Fruit and Organic Frozen Fruit
Ice cream	Organic Banana-based Ice Cream

Fourth Food to Avoid: Processed Foods

Any food that comes in a box, bag, or can, which has a mile long list of ingredients, that can sit unrefrigerated for days, is not good for you. If you have trouble pronouncing an ingredient, it is most likely not good for you.

Trans fats, or partially hydrogenated oils, became popular because they kept cakes, doughnuts, french fries, and cookies fresh longer and feel less greasy. But these artificial oils are just a processed vegetable oil that is solidified. These lead to an increase in cholesterol and inflammation. Common culprits that you have heard of are margarine and Crisco (watch out for partially hydrogenated oil in peanut butter - it should only contain peanuts!)

Excitotoxins, such as MSG (monosodium glutamate), corn protein, glutamate, gelatin, wheat protein, yeast extract, and autolyzed yeast, are used for flavoring and can cause all sorts of problems like asthma, autism, ADD/ADHD, hyperactivity, and diabetes. The common culprits to avoid that contain excitotoxins are frozen meals, canned soups, chips, crackers, sauces, dressings, candy, gum, soda, and CHILDREN's snack food and BABY food.

Fifth Food to Avoid: Genetically Modified Organisms (GMOs), Pesticides, and Fertilizers

Genetically Modified Organisms (GMOs) are simply foods or organisms that have been altered from their natural state to help combat heavy pesticide use, extreme temperatures, resist disease, and/or to battle insects. GMO labeling is required in 64 countries, but the United States and Canada do not require it because of corporate pressure.

The most common GMO plants are corn, soybeans, cotton, potato, alfalfa, canola, papaya, squash, apple, and sugar beet. According to TIME magazine more than 90% of all soybean, cotton, and corn acreage in the US is used to grow genetically engineered crops.

20 years ago, no genetically modified foods existed.

So what is the big deal with GMO's?

Crops are not genetically modified for nutritional reasons. They're modified for economic reasons. Faster growth, with pesticide resistance so they can add more pesticides during growth. Pesticide use continues to rise due to the creation of superweeds and hard-to-kill insects that are becoming resistant to pesticides.

Fertilizers are also used to provide much needed nutrients to soils that used to exist prior to the use of pesticides. Multiple USDA studies reveal that the food currently grown on America's chemical-intensive factory farms contain drastically less vitamins and essential minerals than the food produced 50 years ago (when pesticides and fertilizers were not used as frequently).

Most food coming from factory farms is nutritionally deficient, laced with pesticides, antibiotics, hormones, harmful bacteria and viruses, genetically modified organisms (GMOs), and toxic chemicals. Factory farms and traditional product from these farms are a hazard to your health.

How to Avoid GMO's, Pesticides, & Fertilizers

Simply buy organic or foods labeled non-GMO, know the farmer you're buying from (like farmer's markets), plant a garden, and eliminate the ten crops listed above from your diet.

For an easy start, go by the Environmental Working Group's Dirty Dozen and Clean Fifteen. However, for the easiest way to think about this just always buy organic, which is what we do.

ALWAYS buy organic when it comes to the Dirty Dozen which includes strawberries, spinach, nectarines, apples, peaches, celery, grapes, pears, cherries, tomatoes, sweet bell peppers, and potatoes. Avoid these items if they are not organic.

The Clean Fifteen should still be bought organic if possible, but they have less pesticide residue compared to other produce. This list includes sweet corn, avocados, pineapple, cabbage, onions, sweet peas, papayas, asparagus, mangoes, eggplant, honeydew melon, kiwi, cantaloupe, cauliflower, and grapefruit.

Pesticide side effects include nausea, vomiting, diarrhea, stomach cramps, headache, dizziness, weakness, confusion, excessive sweating, chills, thirst, chest pains, difficulty breathing, cramps in your muscles, and aches all over your body

#3 Way To Reduce Inflammation: Give Your Cells Oxygen

We can all agree, we need oxygen to live. Try holding your breath for 30 seconds and depriving yourself of oxygen. What happens? Your body goes into a shocked state and starts to make every effort to take another breath.

What you are eating is possibly doing this to the rest of your body without you knowing it. You have 100 trillion cells that rely on oxygen on a daily basis. The cells of your body are in constant regeneration, meaning they die and then new ones are created. As each new cell is built, the body seeks proper building materials from which to construct each cell. These building materials are what you put into your body.

The number one thing that determines how operational and healthy these cells will be is the fuel that they are given, which is also known as the food you eat.

The expression, "you are what you eat" will take on a whole new meaning after this section.

The cells in your body (each individual cell of the 100 trillion that you have) is like a city, according to E.G. Heinrich. It is full of activity. Water, oxygen, minerals, and amino acids (parts of protein) are the primary parts of the inside of the cell. This is where life-sustaining processes mainly occur. Cell membranes are the "walls" around the city that allow things in and out, while protecting the cells. These cell membranes are becoming unhealthy by the unhealthy oils you are eating. This includes trans fat (likely from the Western diet of fried and processed foods) and vegetable oils (corn, soybean, canola). These unhealthy oils are resistive to oxygen and therefore your cells are starved of oxygen leading to a chronic inflammatory state.

Short term you may not notice a difference, but long term this creates diseases like heart disease, diabetes, high cholesterol, arthritis, dry eyes, and more. According to Brian Peskin, all disease involves a lack of oxygen at the cellular level. If oxygen is in the cell, you will have good health. Nobel Prize Winner Dr. Warburg stated that if a cell is denied 60% of its oxygen requirements, then cancer can occur.

The great news about this is that your cells regenerate every two days to six months (depending on which part of the body we're discussing). Your body grows news cells in the eye every two days, new skin in six weeks, a new liver in eight weeks, new nerve cells in a period of months. As each new cell is built, the body seeks proper building materials from which to construct the cell. If it cannot find these, it will create unhealthy cells, deprived of oxygen.

The body has an incredible ability to heal itself, IF provided with the proper nutrition and building blocks. So starting today you can make changes that lead to a healthier, more fulfilling lifestyle that isn't riddled with disease and pain.

These changes include avoiding (at all costs) eating oxygen-resistive oils, like corn, canola, or soybean oil and consume instead oxygen-enabling oils such as healthy omega-3 (high quality fish oil or flaxseed oil) and omega-6 (evening primrose oil or black currant seed oil).

Oils to Avoid are Modern Vegetable Oils (especially after being heated):

- Margarine
- Shortening (Crisco)
- Fake Butter Substitutes (I Can't Believe It's Not Butter)
- Corn Oil
- Soybean Oil
- Canola Oil
- "Vegetable" Oil
- Peanut Oil
- Cottonseed Oil
- Grapeseed Oil

Foods to Avoid Unhealthy Omega-6's

- All the oils listed above
- ANY fried foods (they fry them in the oils above)
- Salad dressing (they use the oils above) - substitute vinegar instead, like balsamic
- Chips
- Fast Food - chicken fingers, french fries, hash browns, chicken nuggets, McDonald's
- Freezer meals
- Cookies, candy, cakes, pastries, muffins, candy bars, etc
- Pork products such as bacon, pork chops, pork loin, ham, etc
- Limit cheeses that are NOT white, but some is okay (see below)

Oils to EAT to Help Reduce Inflammation

These foods with healthy oils listed below help rebuild your cells into healthier cells able to transfer oxygen and reduce inflammation and disease. These healthier oils can also cross the blood/brain and blood/eye barriers, which means they will benefit both the brain and eye more, helping with dry eye.

When using an oil in cooking (it is never recommended to heat an oil), use only an **Organic, Virgin, Cold-Pressed <u>Coconut Oil</u>**.

If you are already a healthy individual (be honest), you should be getting a 2:1 ratio of healthy omega-6 to healthy omega-3. However, if you suffer from numerous diseases, are overweight, or eat terribly, you should start by shifting your diet first (which we'll discuss more in later sections and come back to this section later as well) and start with a ratio 4:1 ratio of healthy omega-6 to healthy omega-3 (some suggest even 8:1 to combat all that "bad" fat you have been eating).

If you start to pay attention to this ratio and you can get it to 4:1, then you will be more than doubling the amount of oxygen that moves from your blood to your cells, which will decrease pain, inflammation, and disease.

This is NOT a short term fix, though, and requires a lifestyle change. What you are doing now is not working and causing you a tremendous amount of pain... FIX IT. It is not up to a doctor to fix your problem, it is on you!

Examples of healthy omega fatty acids:

- **Healthy Vegetarian Omega-6's**
    - Avocado (15:1 omega-6 to omega-3 ratio)
    - Flaxseed oil (or <u>ground</u>)
    - <u>Chia seeds</u>
    - <u>Evening primrose oil</u>
    - Black currant seed oil
    - <u>Walnuts</u>
    - <u>Almonds</u>
        - <u>Almond butter</u>
    - <u>Sunflower seeds</u>
        - <u>Sunflower seed butter</u>
    - <u>Sesame seeds</u>
    - <u>Pine nuts</u>
    - <u>Brazil nuts</u>
    - <u>Pecans</u>

- o Pumpkin seeds
- o Hemp seeds
- **Healthy Vegetarian Omega-3's**
  - o Avocado (15:1 omega-6 to omega-3 ratio)
  - o Flaxseed oil (or ground)
  - o Chia seeds
  - o Evening primrose oil
  - o Black currant seed oil
  - o Walnuts
  - o Almonds
    - Almond butter
  - o Sunflower seeds
    - Sunflower seed butter
  - o Sesame seeds
  - o Pine nuts
  - o Brazil nuts
  - o Pecans
  - o Pumpkin seeds
  - o Hemp seeds
  - o Fresh basil
  - o Dried oregano
  - o Cloves
  - o Canned grape leaves
- **Healthy Meat Omega-6**
  - o Organic, free-range eggs
  - o Organic cheese - try to stick to WHITE cheese such as cottage cheese, parmesan, goat cheese, gruyere
  - o Organic whole milk
  - o Organic, grass-fed butter
  - o Organic, grass-fed, free-range beef
  - o Organic, grass-fed, free-range poultry
- **Healthy Meat Omega-3**
  - o High quality fish (make sure it's wild)
    - Mackerel
    - Wild Alaskan salmon

- Herring
- Wild caught tuna
- Sardines

#4 Way To Reduce Inflammation: Essential Minerals

Magnesium is one of the most essential minerals needed by the body, yet it is the most lacking mineral in the human diet. Unfortunately with the current farming practices, it has been stripped from the soil so much that we now need to supplement. A study of almost 4,000 postmenopausal women shows that 100 mg of magnesium per day was associated with a significant reduction in various inflammatory markers.

A good way to help replace essential minerals is supplementation. Another way is replacing all the table salt in your house with Celtic Sea Salt, which contains 82 trace minerals.

Nuts and vegetables are also great way to increase your essential minerals consumption. These foods include: pumpkin seeds, sunflower seeds, almonds, hazelnut, Brazil nuts, spinach, kale, sweet potatoes, peppers, sea vegetables, onions, asparagus, cabbage, brussel sprouts, broccoli, kale, turnips, beans,

#5 Way To Reduce Inflammation: Vitamin Deficiency

Vitamin A is one of the largest vitamin deficiencies worldwide. It has a vital role as an anti-inflammatory agent and can be obtained sufficiently through supplementation.

Low Vitamin B6 is associated with inflammation according to WebMD. This can be found naturally in legumes and vegetables. Studies show that people with the highest inflammation have the lowest levels of vitamin B6 in their blood. Your body excretes any excess B vitamins therefore it is never retained.

Vitamin C plays a vital role in relieving inflammation, boosting your immune system, and protecting your joints. Your body excretes any excess vitamin C therefore it is never retained.

Vitamin D has been shown to inhibit the inflammatory cascade, therefore reducing inflammation.

Eating a well balanced diet of fruits, vegetables, grains, and legumes, you will not have much of a vitamin deficiency. Also supplementation with a good multivitamin and B complex will help with this (#8 below).

#6 Way To Reduce Inflammation: Electron Deficiency

Grounding is the practice of getting back in touch with the naturally negative charged free electrons that the earth has. Research has shown that if you place your bare feet on the ground (grass, beach, ocean... not concrete) after injury, electrons from the earth will migrate into your body and spread through your tissues.

During injury when our immune system responds, it releases many chemicals that create an inflammatory cascade. One chemical released is reactive oxygen species, or free radicals, which can leak into healthy tissue causing inflammation in non-injured tissue. When grounding, electrons from the earth travel to this area and naturally bind to these free radicals, neutralizing them and making them harmless.

This is a process that is CONSTANTLY going on in your body, so grounding daily is very beneficial. You have probably heard people talk about the power of the beach and ocean? That is because we finally take our rubber-soled, electron-blocking shoes off and walk barefoot. You can also sit outside with your barefeet in the grass.

According to the Journal of Environmental and Public Health, grounding benefits can include better sleep and reduced pain (from decreased inflammation).

#7 Way To Reduce Inflammation: Sleep

Most repair and regeneration occurs in our body when we sleep. When we sleep we have more energy for creating new, healthier cells (if following a plant-based diet) to replace the unhealthy cells that no longer work as efficiently. Try to get at least seven hours of sleep per night, and listen to your body!

#8 Way To Reduce Inflammation: Supplementation

- **Multivitamin**
  - o For women, we recommend <u>My Kind Organics Garden of Life Multivitamin for Women</u>
  - o For men, we recommend <u>My Kind Organics Garden of Life Multivitamin for Men</u>
- **Organic Evening Primrose Oil** (Omega-6) 4 grams loading dose daily for 3 months, then 2 grams daily for maintenance
  - o We recommend <u>Health From The Sun Organic, Cold Pressed, Evening Primrose Oil</u>
- **Organic Flaxseed Oil, or Fish Oil** (Omega-3) 1 gram daily
  - o We recommend <u>Heyedrate Omega-3 for Dry Eye</u>

- **Probiotics**
  - We recommend <u>Organifi Biotic Balance Probiotic</u>
- **Vitamin B Complex**
  - We recommend <u>Garden of Life B Complex with Folate</u>
- **Vitamin C** and **Vitamin E**
  - We recommend <u>Eye Love Ocular Health Formula</u>
- **Phytochemicals** (Carotenoids): Lutein, Zeaxanthin, Astaxanthin
  - We recommend <u>Eye Love Ocular Health Formula</u>

Chapter 5 - Simple Meal Preparation

Breakfast and Lunch Green Smoothie Chart

We often eat a green smoothie for breakfast and lunch, which will start your day with a ton of antioxidants, nutrients, vitamins, minerals, and alkalizing foods to give your body a boost and make you feel full and productive. It will also give you a boost after lunch and NOT that tired, food "coma" feeling that you usually have.

GREEN SMOOTHIE CHART

Some Helpful Tips (**Makes 1 large blender/2 servings**)

- For the liquid base, you want 1 cup of filtered water and 1 cup of one of the following: Coconut Water, Coconut Milk, or Almond Milk
- Blend in stages - liquid + greens first, then add everything else (we just throw it all together)
- Organic Frozen Fruit is great for the second column. Then you do not need to add ice.
- Avoid sugar and artificial sweeteners (use bananas, mango, apples, pears, dates instead)
- Make them ahead of time for lunches, snacks, and when you need a quick fix.
- T. = Tablespoon (you can use a normal spoon from your kitchen)

Pick Yours Greens 2-3 cups total 2-3 handfuls	Pick 2 For Flavor 2-3 cups total	Pick 2 Healthy Fats	Flavor Enhancers & Health Boosters
Spinach	Strawberries	½ Avocado	1 Scoop Protein Powder
Kale	Blueberries	2-3 T. Flax Seeds	1 Scoop Greens Powder
Hearts of Romaine	Blackberries	2-3 T. Chia Seeds	(or an All-In-One Powder)
Raw Broccoli	Raspberries	2-3 T. Hemp Seeds	
Bok Choy	Mango	1 T. Coconut Oil	
Swiss Chard	Banana	1 -2 T. Almond Butter	OPTIONAL
Collards	No Sugar Added Pitted Dates	½ cup Walnuts	½ cup Frozen Cauliflower
Dandelion	No Sugar Added Apricots	½ cup Almonds	1-2 T. Cacao Powder
Boston Lettuce	No Sugar Added Raisins	½ cup Sunflower Seeds	1-2 T. Cinnamon
	Grapes	½ cup Sesame Seeds	1-2 T. Acai Powder'
	Apple	½ cup Pine Nuts	1 T. Celtic Sea Salt
	Peeled Orange	½ cup Brazil Nuts	1-2 T. Nutritional Yeast
	Melon	½ cup Pecans	1-2 T. Local Honey
	Pineapple	½ cup Pumpkin Seeds	½ Lemon Squeezed
	Cucumber		½ Lime Squeezed
	Kiwi		1 t. of various spices like Turmeric, Ginger, Cloves
	Carrot		
	Peaches		
	Papaya		
	Celery		
	Pear		

Other Lunch Ideas

We usually do a green smoothie for lunch as well, but wanted to give you some other options. If we don't eat a green smoothie for lunch, we usually stick with a salad or vegetarian yogurt mixture.

LUNCH SALAD CHART (serves 1)

Some Helpful Tips
- ALWAYS buy organic when possible.
- An example is with spinach. You lose almost 90% of nutrients when buying traditional spinach vs organic spinach. Plus there are over 52 pesticides found on traditional spinach.
- For Dressing, do NOT use ready-made dressing as they contain bad fats. Just use the vinegar of your choice (I love putting a little hot sauce on as well)
- Balsamic Vinegar
- Local Honey + Mustard
- Tabasco Sauce or Frank's Red Hot Sauce
- Add a little fruit to enhance the flavor as well (just not too much)
- Apples slices, strawberries, blueberries, blackberries, no sugar added pitted dates, dried apricots, or raisins
- Save Meat (if you must eat it) for dinner only... Your body will thank you!
- T. = Tablespoon (You can use a normal spoon from your kitchen)

Pick Yours Greens 2-3 cups total	Proteins 1 cup total	Pick 1-2 Healthy Fats	Pick 1-5 Veggies NO LIMIT
Spinach	**BEANS - Pick 1**	½ Avocado	Broccoli
Kale	Navy Beans	2-3 T. Flax Seeds	Tomato
Hearts of Romaine	Chickpeas	2-3 T. Chia Seeds	Carrots
Raw Broccoli	Black Beans	2-3 T. Hemp Seeds	Celery
Bok Choy	Cannellini Beans	½ cup Walnuts	Asparagus
Swiss Chard	Red Kidney Beans	½ cup Almonds	Green Beans
Collards	Lentils	½ cup Sunflower Seeds	Corn
Dandelion	Firm tofu	½ cup Sesame Seeds	Cauliflower
Boston Lettuce	Edamame	½ cup Pine Nuts	Cucumber
		½ cup Brazil Nuts	Mushrooms
	GRAINS - Pick 1	½ cup Pecans	Peppers
	Quinoa	½ cup Pumpkin Seeds	Zucchini
	Millet		Squash
	Spelt		Peas
	Brown Rice		Sweet Potato
	Wild Rice		Nori
	Farro		Hijiki
	Barley		Arame
	Oats		
	Bulgar		

LUNCH YOGURT CHART (serves 1)

Some Helpful Tips
- Do NOT buy the flavored yogurt as it contains a TON of artificial sugars and sweeteners
- T. = Tablespoon (You can use a normal spoon from your kitchen)

Pick Your Yogurt ½ to 1 cup	Pick 2 For Flavor ½ to 1 cup total	Pick 1-2 Healthy Fats	Flavor Enhancers & Health Boosters
Greek Yogurt Coconut Yogurt Soy Yogurt (NO FLAVOR, PLAIN)	Strawberries Blueberries Blackberries Raspberries Mango Banana No Sugar Added Pitted Dates No Sugar Added Apricots No Sugar Added Raisins Grapes Apple Peeled Orange Melon Pineapple Cucumber Kiwi Carrot Peaches Papaya Celery Pear	½ Avocado 2-3 T. Flax Seeds 2-3 T. Chia Seeds 2-3 T. Hemp Seeds ½ cup Walnuts ½ cup Almonds ½ cup Sunflower Seeds ½ cup Sesame Seeds ½ cup Pine Nuts ½ cup Brazil Nuts ½ cup Pecans ½ cup Pumpkin Seeds	1 Scoop Protein Powder 1 Scoop Greens Powder (or an All-In-One Powder) OPTIONAL 1-2 T. Cacao Powder 1-2 T. Cinnamon 1-2 T. Acai Powder' 1 T. Celtic Sea Salt 1-2 T. Nutritional Yeast 1-2 T. Local Honey ½ Lemon Squeezed ½ Lime Squeezed 1 t. of various spices like Turmeric, Ginger, Cloves

Ideas for Dinner

This chart can be made into stir-fry, soup, or eaten raw (except meat) as in a salad or bowl.

DINNER CHART (serves 1)

Some Helpful Tips
- Save Meat (if you must eat it) for dinner only... Your body will thank you!
- Soup? Put all these ingredients in a crock pot or regular pot and add vegetable broth for a tasty soup
  - Add fermented Miso paste for probiotic addition, just make sure it's made from barley and aged at least 2 years (the powdered stuff isn't the same).
- Stir-Fry? Put all these ingredients in a pan and fry them up! Serve with rice or quinoa.
- T. = Tablespoon (You can use a normal spoon from your kitchen)
- Meat (not recommended) can be substituted in the bean section below
  - Organic, grass-fed, free range meat: Lean ground turkey, beef, or chicken
  - Wild salmon, wild tuna, or wild shrimp
  - Organic, free-range eggs (hard-boiled, scrambled, over-easy)

Base of Greens 2-3 cups total Cooked or Raw	Proteins 1-2 cups total	Pick 1-2 Healthy Fats	Pick 1-5 Veggies NO LIMIT
Spinach	**BEANS - Pick 1**	2-3 T. Flax Seeds	Broccoli
Kale	Navy Beans	2-3 T. Chia Seeds	Tomato
Hearts of Romaine	Chickpeas	2-3 T. Hemp Seeds	Carrots
Raw Broccoli	Black Beans	½ cup Walnuts	Celery
Bok Choy	Cannellini Beans	½ cup Almonds	Asparagus
Swiss Chard	Red Kidney	½ cup Sunflower Seeds	Green Beans
Collards	Beans	½ cup Sesame Seeds	Corn
Dandelion	Lentils	½ cup Pine Nuts	Cauliflower
Boston Lettuce	Firm tofu	½ cup Brazil Nuts	Cucumber
Mustard Greens	Edamame	½ cup Pecans	Mushrooms
Watercress		½ cup Pumpkin Seeds	Peppers
	GRAINS - Pick 1		Zucchini
	Quinoa		Squash
	Millet		Peas
	Spelt		Sweet Potato
	Brown Rice		Nori
	Wild Rice		Hijiki
	Farro		Arame
	Barley		Wakame
	Oats		Kombu
	Bulgar		

Ideas for Snacks

Snacking can also be a healthy choice when done smart. Some of our favorite snacks include:

- Vegetables like broccoli, carrots, celery, and cauliflower dipped in hummus
- Homemade kale chips (put kale in the oven and bake until crisp)
- Homemade corn tortilla chips (put corn tortilla sliced up in the oven until crisp) and dip into guacamole
- Apples, peaches, or other fruits
- Nuts like walnuts, almonds, sunflower seeds, sesame seeds, pine nuts, Brazil nuts, pecans, pumpkin seeds
- Spoonful of almond butter, sunflower seed butter

Ideas for Desserts

There are SO many sweet desserts in nature, you just choose to reach for the cookies, cakes, brownies, candy, and ice cream instead. What about all the fruits of this world? Frozen organic grapes, strawberries, blueberries or fresh, organic, ripe blackberries, cherries, or raspberries.

Nature's dessert is fruit, feel free to indulge in moderation when a sweet tooth craving hits!

Banana "ice cream" is very easy to make. Take a banana and slice it up. Place in freezer for 24 hours. Put slices along with a splash of almond milk into a food processer and blend until smooth, adding almond milk as needed. Add any healthy flavor boosters to make the flavor you want. This includes protein powder, greens powder, cacao powder, cinnamon, acai powder, local honey, and lemon or lime squeezed. You can also add other frozen fruit, like blueberries.

Chapter 6 - Hydration and Drinking Plenty of Water

Treatment for ALL disease should start with drinking plenty of water daily. Seventy-five percent (75%!!!) of us walk around dehydrated. You should be carrying around a reusable <u>water bottle</u> with you at all times (do yourself and our planet a favor and avoid disposable plastic water bottles!). Follow the motto, if you think, drink! This means that every time you think about drinking water, you should take a drink. We have a survival mechanism that tells us we are starting to get thirsty before we even do.

What Dehydration Causes...

Dehydration can cause a list of ailments and symptoms that are very similar to disease. A lot of people who are just dehydrated are diagnosed with disease, when a simple glass of water (or ten glasses) can help eliminate these symptoms. Dehydration can cause dry eye, brain fog and fatigue, disease, sickness, and overall malaise. Sound familiar? Get drinking!

Symptoms of dehydration include
- Thirst
- Dry mouth
- Fatigue
- Decreased urination or deep yellow urine
- Headache
- Dizziness

How Much to Drink?

This obviously depends on the size of the person, but a typical recommended dose per day is 2 liters, which is about 10-8 ounce glasses of water (think dinner glasses). 10 glasses of water per day may sound daunting, but I assure you, with a system and reusable water bottle in place, it is easy to surpass that.

Drink great quality water that is free of heavy metals (often found in tap water). Make sure you have a heavy duty filter. Most refrigerator filters do not filter out everything but are a good start. We purchased and recommend the <u>BIG Berkey water filtration</u> countertop unit. You can also have an in-house filtration system installed under your sink.

Avoid beverages and foods which have diuretic effects such as coffee, caffeinated teas (limit to less than 2 cups per day), and alcohol (less than 1 standard drink per day). If you must have your caffeine, make sure you're drinking at least that same amount of water right after to avoid dehydration.

Side note: Dr. Travis Zigler drinks 2 liters right after waking up to hyper-hydrate (more on this later). Dr. Jenna drinks at least 3-32 ounce water bottles full daily, spacing it out throughout her day (1 full bottle is consumed before she eats anything that day).

Hyper-Hydration & The Effects of Proper Hydration

Hyper-hydration is a term given to drinking a lot of water in a short period of time to flush the body with water. Wake up with a hyper-hydration session of 16 to 32 ounces of water (2 to 4 cups, 0.5 to 1.0 liters). YES, you can add a squeeze of lemon or apple cider vinegar to your water for enhanced effects. It will take your body a few days to adjust to drinking this much first thing, but the effects are well worth it!

Flushing the body with water and staying properly hydrated has numerous effects on the body including boosting your metabolism by 30-50% for the next two hours (which is like working out). It will flush your circulatory and lymphatic system of toxins accumulated in the body throughout the day before, as water is the purge vehicle for toxins.

Along with flushing the body of these toxins, proper hydration lowers the noise in your body and connects your mind to your body (less brain fog = more clarity). You will feel the effects of hydration after 3-days of using hyper-hydration in the morning. You will feel clearer and more alive than ever before.

Three-Step System To Keep Hydrated
1. Drink 16 to 32 ounces (0.5 to 1.0 liters) of water right after waking up, before eating.
   o Benefits: purge toxins, flush the circulatory & lymphatic system, and boost metabolism
2. Keep close proximity to water
   o Benefits: everytime you look at your bottle, you will take a drink
3. If you think, drink!
   o Benefits: being hydrated all day leads to a 30 to 50% increase in metabolism

ACTION ITEMS

1. Start the Three-Step System AS SOON AS POSSIBLE.

2. Purchase a <u>32 ounce (or larger) water bottle</u> and keep it near you at all times. Whenever you look at your water bottle, take a drink.

3. Start hyperhydration right when you wake up and do this before your first meal.

4. Purchase a <u>Camelback Backpack</u> (more to come on this) for working out.

5. Purchase a <u>BIG Berkey Water Filtration Kit</u> to decrease toxins in your drinking water.

Chapter 7 - Exercise To Eliminate Disease

Treatment for ALL disease should start with drinking plenty of water and exercising daily. According to <u>CBS News</u>, 80-90% of adults and teens do not exercise. That is 8-9 out of every 10 people that do NOT exercise. No wonder health care costs are rising and disease is rampant in the United States. The biggest problem we see as practitioners is the advice we give our patients about diet and exercise are completely ignored and patients just want to feel relief from the symptoms of the disease. A disease is your body's way of telling you that you are doing something wrong (most likely following a Western diet and failing to exercise).

With that being said, DO NOT RELY ON YOUR PRACTITIONER TO CURE YOUR DISEASE. This is up to YOU and YOU alone. You can choose today to start eating better, exercising daily, and healing your body from the inside out.

What Are Some of the Benefits of Exercise?

Exercise is one of the most beneficial activities you can engage in to improve your life, from your mood to your sex drive. A dopamine hit will come across you and last throughout the day. Dopamine is responsible for increasing calmness, awareness, and your presence in life while decreasing anxiety, depression, anger, and more. Some other benefits of exercise include the following according to the <u>Mayo Clinic</u>:

- Controls and helps you lose weight
- Combats health conditions and disease
- Improves your mood and combats depression
- Boosts energy levels
- Promotes better sleep
- Puts the spark back into your sex life!

What a Sedentary Lifestyle Causes…

Lack of physical activity can cause a list of ailments and symptoms which increase your risk for developing disease. Sedentary lifestyles causes an extreme dive opposite of those exercise-enhancing benefits above. According to <u>Men's Health</u>, these are:

- Depression, anxiety, restlessness, hopelessness, or even fatigue
- SIGNIFICANT increased risk of cancer
- Memory loss
- Increased blood sugar and risk for diabetes

- No more sex… Or at least a decreased sex drive :(
- Terrible sleep
- Increased back pain (especially lower back)

How Much to Exercise?

This depends on the shape that you are in, but we shoot for about 210 minutes of exercise per week (30 minutes per day). we know this sounds like a daunting task, but we are going to give you a complete action plan to get to 30 minutes per day. We now do 45-60 minutes per day, six days per week. WE DIDN'T START HERE. We gradually worked our way up to it and we blocked off time every morning to work out.

Exercise Plan If You Are Currently NOT Exercising

How do you eat an elephant? It is a pretty big task that would be tough, but you do it ONE BITE AT A TIME!

- **Week one** is all about getting back into the routine or creating a routine
    - Start waking up an hour earlier, hyper-hydrating, and going on a five minute **brisk** walk (or as long as you can)
    - Do this daily (Pain permitting, and soreness is not pain. Walk through the soreness.)
    - FIVE MINUTES PER DAY is all you need to get a habit started.
- **Week two through six** is all about adding time
    - Add five minutes per week.
        - Week two = 10 minutes of brisk walking per day
        - Week three = 15 minutes of brisk walking per day
        - Week four = 20 minutes of brisk walking per day
        - Week five = 25 minutes of brisk walking per day
        - Week six = 30 minutes of brisk walking per day
- **After week six,** maintain this 30 minutes per day at the VERY LEAST
    - If you can, continue adding five minutes per week until you get to 60 minutes per day

What we see with our patients that start doing this is they can't stop and exercise becomes an addiction, but a good one. We have seen overweight 50 year olds lose 100 pounds and walk a half marathon within a year of starting this.

Exercise Plan If You Are Currently Exercising

Keep up the good work. See how you stack up against 210 minutes per week and try to get there if you are not already there. You are on the right path.

Meet Beth (True Story)

Beth was a patient of ours who was always cheerful and full of life. Beth was about 210 pounds and 55 years old. She did not exercise or eat well. One night she fainted in her house. She was rushed to the hospital with a blood sugar of over 700 and on the verge of dying. Beth did survive and decided she was going to take matters into her own hands.

She completely changed her diet, eliminating all processed foods (breads, cereals, processed meats) and started an exercise program. In 90 days, she was able to lose 30 pounds and is feeling better than ever. We are so thrilled! She was a diabetic at the ER visit, but is now almost medication free!

This is the power of diet, hydration, and exercise.

Chapter 8 - Eyelids... One of the Major Keys to Successful Dry Eye Management!

Eyelids are more complex than they appear with the naked eye. Your eyelids contain millions of bacteria living on the surface that help keep your eyelids in a normal state. There are also many glands that secrete oils and tears on to your eyes, keeping them comfortable. If any of this becomes disrupted, dry eyes and eyelids can lead to irritation, inflammation, redness, and more uncomfortable situations. This is known as a condition called blepharitis.

What Are Meibomian Glands

Meibomian glands are located on the posterior or back surface of your eyelid. Their primary responsibility is to secrete an oil called meibum into the eye which prevents your tears from evaporating. This leads to more comfortable and less dry eyes. If meibomian glands are disrupted in any way, it can lead to meibomian gland dysfunction (MGD), which results in symptoms of dry eyes, grittiness, irritation, inflammation, redness, and that feeling like you have "sand in your eye."

NERD ALERT → Meibomian glands have little oil producing factories, called acini, that produce oil. Acini release the oil into the meibomian gland and, with the help of the eyelid muscle (the orbicularis oculi), milks the oil down the gland and out the opening called the terminal duct. This occurs every time you blink. The oil is then released onto the eye's surface to help prevent evaporation of your tears.

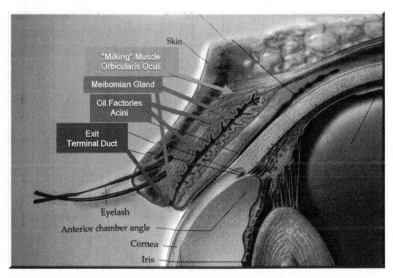

What is Meibomian Gland Dysfunction?

Meibomian gland dysfunction (MGD), or posterior blepharitis, occurs when any part of the process discussed above is dysfunctional. The muscle can lose its function, the oil factories can stop working, and the opening can become clogged. Treatment is directed at helping avoid these problems and will be discussed below.

MGD Symptoms and Signs

Meibomian gland dysfunction (MGD) is going to cause the following signs and symptoms of blepharitis:

- Red, inflamed eyes
- Itchy eyes
- Gritty eyes
- Irritated eyes
- Dry eyes

MGD Treatment

Meibomian gland dysfunction treatment can be as simple as warm compresses at home (which are shown to provide symptom relief), to diet changes and supplements, to in-office procedures such as IPL, MiboFlo, or Lipiflow.

Warm Compresses

Warm compresses are best performed with a mask that is specifically formulated for dry eye, like our Heyedrate Dry Eye Warm Compress, which contains flaxseed and lavender in a silk mask. You can also make a warm compress by taking dry rice or whole flax seed and putting it into a clean sock.

Instructions for our Home Spa Therapy (aka Warm Compresses)

1. Microwave the Heyedrate Dry Eye Warm Compress for 20 seconds.
2. Shake the mask to ensure even heating.
3. Test on the inside of your wrist for temperature as to not burn the eyelids.
4. Place over closed eyes and tie onto head.
5. RELAX.... For 20 minutes!

We recommend applying warm compresses at least every night, but you cannot overdose, so feel free to do it as often as you want for symptom relief. More recent studies have shown that warm compresses are not as effective as other treatment options for meibomian gland dysfunction, but we still consider it a staple in the routine of our dry eye patients. Other treatment options are more expensive, but not as convenient. We will discuss these briefly below and in more detail later.

Meibomian Gland Expression After Warm Compresses

Meibomian gland expression is the process of expressing the meibomian glands after heating. Heating up your meibomian glands helps turn the oil into more of a liquid (think of placing a stick of butter on the stove... it melts). After doing this you can milk the glands by rolling a q-tip starting away from your eyelid margin and rolling towards it (or you can use your finger).

After you perform your warm compresses and meibomian gland expression, it is essential to clean your eyelids with a great lid scrub to eliminate all the exfoliated oil from the surface. Heyedrate Lid & Lash Cleanser is the lid scrub we recommend in our clinic. This spray is a natural antiseptic and mimics your body's natural ability to heal. It is free of any harsh chemicals, alcohol, parabens, sulfates, or other preservatives. It is great for all skin types as it does not clog pores and is hypoallergenic. It is also vegan, natural, and organic. Another similar product that is prescription and just as effective is Avenova. We do NOT recommend products like baby shampoo, as was used commonly in the past.

Other MGD Treatments

Lipiflow

Lipiflow applies heat to the inside of the eyelids while simultaneously applying a pulsation to the outer eyelids. This helps to liquefy meibum (oil) and express the meibomian glands at the same time. This procedure usually lasts about 15 minutes.

MiBo Thermoflo

Treating the outer eyelids only, this is very similar to a Lipiflow procedure. MiBo Thermoflo is also a spa-like setting that delivers consistent heat for ten minutes, which will lead to a melting of hardened oil leading to less symptoms and signs of meibomian gland dysfunction. This is usually more affordable than Lipiflow.

IPL (Intense Pulsed Light) Therapy

Originally used as a treatment for Rosacea, patients that were having IPL, or Intense Pulsed Light Therapy, on their skin condition noticed improvement in their dry eye symptoms. IPL is also used for laser hair removal. IPL is brief, powerful bursts of light that cause changes in the blood vessels near the surface of the skin, which raise the skin's temperature, and eliminates problematic flora (bacteria) on the skin and eyes. For meibomian gland dysfunction, the increase in temperature acts like the world's best warm compress and helps eliminate stagnate oil from the glands. It will also decrease inflammation from the treatment area due to changes in the blood vessels.

Warm compresses should still be done in conjunction with these in office procedures. Another great treatment option are omega-3 fatty acids, which will be discussed in depth in the next section.

What is Blepharitis?

Blepharitis is, by definition, an inflammation of the eyelids. There are two different types of blepharitis: anterior (front) and posterior (back) blepharitis which is location dependant. Anterior blepharitis is sometimes called Staph Blepharitis as it is an overgrowth of the normal *Staphylococcus Aureus* that lives on our eyelids. Posterior blepharitis is also called meibomian gland dysfunction (MGD), which we will discuss in the next section.

Anterior Blepharitis Symptoms and Signs

Anterior blepharitis, like stated above, tends to be more bacterial-related. We have normal bacteria that live on our eyelids that can become overpopulated. When this occurs, it is going to cause the following signs and symptoms of blepharitis:

- Red, inflamed eyelids
- Itchy eyelids
- Lids stuck shut upon awakening
- Dandruff on the eyelashes
- Irritated eyelids
- Dry eyes

Blepharitis Treatment With Lid Scrubs

If you have these signs and symptoms, treatment is simply keeping your eyelids cleaner with a lid scrub, like Heyedrate Lid & Lash Cleanser. This spray is a natural antiseptic and mimics your body's natural ability to heal. It is free of any harsh chemicals, alcohol, parabens, sulfates, or other preservatives. It is great for all skin types as it does not clog pores and is hypoallergenic. It is also vegan, natural, and organic.

Heyedrate Lid & Lash Cleanser will help keep your eyelids and eyelashes clean without irritating your skin.

What Eyelid Hygiene NOT to Use?

In the 90's and early 00's, it was common practice for eye care practitioners to prescribe baby shampoo as eyelid hygiene. With <u>further research</u> into this, it has been shown to actually make your eyelids WORSE! Baby shampoo contains a mild detergent which may cause irritation to the eyes. It was not designed for eyelid use. With the availability of better products on the market, you owe it to yourself to upgrade and treat your eyelids right!

How Often Should You Do Lid Scrubs?

We recommend performing lid scrubs two times per day. If your skin becomes dry from this, then reduce to once per day. Check out both Dr. Jenna Zigler and Dr. Travis Zigler's eyelid regimen below.

What Are Demodex

Demodex are tiny mites found in or near hair follicles. They are most commonly found on the face and around the eyelashes. They are usually about 0.3 mm long, have eight legs, and their body is covered in scales for anchoring into a hair follicle. They eat skin cells and oils which accumulate in hair follicles. Demodex is mostly nocturnal and can be transferred via contact. Itchy yet?!

Infestation is very common, especially in the elderly, and usually does not cause symptoms, but skin disease can develop from demodex. The are considered parasitic, however most of the time no adverse symptoms are observed.

Demodex Symptoms and Signs

If your immune system is compromised or if the mite population grows uncontrollably, then symptoms can develop. Symptoms include:

- Red, inflamed eyelids
- Itchy eyelids
- Blepharitis
- Dandruff on eyelashes
- Itchy eyes
- Gritty eyes
- Irritated eyes
- Dry eyes

Demodex Treatment

Using a tea tree based product on your hair, face, and eyelashes every day helps with prevention and elimination of demodex. Click here to watch my video in the shower to see how I prevent demodex. I use Heyedrate Handmade Organic Tea Tree Oil Soap for my hair, body, and face. It helps reduce my eczema, dandruff, and prevents/kills demodex. If you have any skin conditions, this could help reduce the symptoms.

Dr. Jenna Zigler's Eyelid Hygiene Regimen

- Morning Routine
    - Upon awakening, apply two sprays of Heyedrate Lid & Lash Cleanser to a cotton ball/round
    - Wipe in a horizontal motion across both upper and lower eyelid five times
    - Allow Heyedrate Lid & Lash Cleanser to dry, NO NEED TO RINSE OFF
- Shower
    - Wash entire body, hair, and face with Heyedrate Tea Tree Oil Soap
- Evening Routine
    - Remove any makeup with oil-based makeup remover
    - Apply a warm compress to the eyes for ten minutes
    - Lid massage and meibomian gland expression
    - Wash face with Heyedrate Tea Tree Oil Soap
    - Apply two to four sprays of Heyedrate Lid & Lash Cleanser to a cotton ball/round
    - Wipe in a horizontal motion across both upper and lower eyelid five times
    - Allow Heyedrate Lid & Lash Cleanser to dry, NO NEED TO RINSE OFF

Dr. Travis Zigler's Eyelid Hygiene Regimen

- Morning Routine
    - Upon awakening, apply two sprays of Heyedrate Lid & Lash Cleanser directly to eyelids
    - Allow Heyedrate Lid & Lash Cleanser to dry, NO NEED TO RINSE OFF
- Shower

- o Wash entire body, hair, and face with <u>Heyedrate Tea Tree Oil Soap</u>
- Evening Routine
  - o Wash face with a <u>Heyedrate Tea Tree Oil Soap</u>
  - o Two to four sprays of <u>Heyedrate Lid & Lash Cleanser</u> directly to closed eyelids
  - o Gently rub in eyelid area
  - o Allow <u>Heyedrate Lid & Lash Cleanser</u> to dry, NO NEED TO RINSE OFF

Chapter 9 - Other Lifestyle Modifications

Although everything mentioned above will create the biggest difference in your dry eye battle, a few other lifestyle modifications should be taken into account.

Lifestyle Modification #1: STOP Smoking

Smoking affects dry eye in two different ways. The most important way is the inhalation of numerous toxins and chemicals that flood your bloodstream with free radicals, which, as discussed above, increases your risk for dry eye, heart disease, and cancer. Secondly, the actual smoke is an eye irritant as well.

I don't need to go into more detail, as smoking has been proven over and over again to cause problems and you have probably heard it ad nauseum. If you smoke, there's never been a better time to quit!

Lifestyle Modification #2: Avoid Fans

Direct wind can cause a lot of irritation, whether it be from air conditioning or heat in your car, overhead or direct fans at home, and natural wind from mother nature. Turn your vents and fans away from your face if you need to have them on.

To block natural wind, wear a great pair of sunglasses that wrap well and provide a barrier of protection.

Lifestyle Modifications #3: Wear Sunglasses

As stated above, find a pair that wraps well and blocks the wind, but any sunglasses are better than none. Make sure you're wearing sunglasses whenever you're outdoors. Sunglasses are not just for sunny days! UV radiation can enter the eye even on cloudy days, and getting into the habit of wearing them means your eyes will always be more comfortable.

Lifestyle Modification #4: Avoid Excessive Phone, Tablet, and Computer Use

The 20-20-20 rule is a simple tool designed to use at work or home to reduce eye strain from viewing a computer or other digital display screen such as cell phones, televisions, and tablets.

Good ergonomics and safety for computer workstation users involves frequent breaks. Computer users must also provide breaks to their eyes. Computer users often look at a computer screen for eight or more hours a day!

The 20-20-20 rule reduces eye fatigue. The worker takes a break from screen time every 20 minutes, then looks at something at least 20 feet away for at least 20 seconds. This activity gives a regular break to the eyes to help avoid eye strain by focusing on distant objects.

It is often hard to start a new habit, especially if it is a healthy one. In order to remember to take eye breaks every 20 minutes, it might be helpful to set the alarm on your cell phone. However, this is distracting if a person works in a cube in close proximity to other people, so an alternative might be to set your timer to vibrate until you get in the habit of naturally taking a short eye strain break every 20 minutes. There are also apps and a Chrome extension that will pop up every 20 minutes to remind you to take a break.

Practice the 20-20-20 rule, even if you're not experiencing eye strain, as it also works as an effective preventative measure.

If you're willing and your schedule permits, you don't need to stop with looking away from the computer screen every 20 minutes. Actually get up and walk around. Grab a cup of coffee or tea. Drinking water may be an even better choice because caffeinated and sugar-laden drinks can dehydrate the body, adding to eye strain by drying out the eyes. Visit a coworker's cube and talk for a few minutes. Make a phone call while walking for a bit outside.

Not only will walking around reduce eye strain, but it keeps a person more active during an otherwise sedentary period, increasing alertness and leading to higher productivity, as well as supporting overall health and wellness.

Blue Light Blocking Glasses

Another way to prevent eyestrain on the computer is to get a pair of blue light blocking lenses for your glasses. Blue light from our computer screen disrupts our sleep patterns, leading to less sleep and less impactful, healing sleep. Having blue light blocking lenses will help reduce this and allow your body to heal more easily at nighttime.

If you wear prescription glasses, talk to your optometrist or wherever you buy glasses about getting a blue-light blocking coating added to your lenses. You can also request a prescription for computer lenses and not have to use your distance prescription on the computer.

Lifestyle Modification #5: Reduce Stress

The next chapter will cover this in more detail!

Chapter 10 - What is Stress?

Adrenaline is pumping through your body, eyes are dilated, palms are sweaty, heartbeat speeds up, muscles tense, breath is short... Sound familiar? This is your body's "fight or flight" response that occurs when you are in a stressful situation. Your nervous system releases hormones that prepare you to fight whatever the offending agent is or to run. This is your body's short-term response to stress and it recovers quickly from this. This is a survival mechanism in the body and does more good than harm.

However if this stress if present over a long period of time (chronic stress), it can lead to more serious health problems. Aging more quickly, decreased immune system, and higher disease prevalence are just a few of the problems that can occur due to long term stress.

What Causes Stress?
- Disability
- Death
- Divorce
- Getting Fired
- Unemployment
- Lack of job satisfaction
- Money
- Chronic disease
- Injury
- Depression, anxiety, anger, grief, low self-esteem or other emotional problems
- Traumatic events like theft, rape, or violence against you
- Natural disasters such as hurricanes, tornadoes, or floods
- But not all stressors are bad
  - Marriage
  - Moving
  - Taking care of family
- **MOST IMPORTANT = YOUR ATTITUDE**
  - **How you view the world**
  - **How you react to a particular situation**
  - **Unrealistic expectations**
  - **This is what I will focus on below**

Short Term Effects of Stress on the Body - "Fight or Flight"

- Dry eyes
- Headache
- Fatigue – feeling tired
- Dilated pupils
- Stiff neck and shoulder pain
- Back pain
- Increased heart rate
- Sweaty palms and feet
- Upset stomach
- Depression

Long Term Effects of Stress on the Body

Chronic stress on the body can cause serious long term health conditions on the body. These include, but are not limited to:

- Dry eyes
- Infertility due to hormone fluctuations and changes
- Heart disease
- Suppressed immune systems
- Muscle pains
- Asthma
- Acne
- Eczema
- Psoriasis
- Anxiety
- Depression

Stress's effects on the blood and circulatory system are what is thought to cause dry eyes. Blood is thicker, blood pressure is increased, and blood supply to extremities (legs, skin, arms) is decreased, which also affects the eyes and brain. This decrease in blood supply is thought to cause dry eyes.

Cause >> Effect

As Tony Robbins says, "What if life is happening FOR us and not TO us?" What this means is that we need to stop thinking that everything that happens in our life is happening TO us. Stop being the victim and reacting to all scenarios. You get to choose how you react to that person cutting you off or your colleague making fun of you. If you start thinking of life happening FOR us, you start to think, what can I learn from this situation to not let it happen again or to improve my life?

Instead of being reactive, be proactive. Choose to not react to the guy cutting you off or the baby crying or the traffic accident that caused you to be late to work (at least you're not in the accident). If something happens to you that is less than pleasant, close your eyes and take a deep breath. Below I will go over the exact technique I use multiple times per day to avoid these problems and stay on the CAUSE side of the equation. This technique can save you from doing something that you will regret for the rest of your life.

What Is Meditation?

According to Merriam-Webster, meditation is to engage in mental exercise (such as concentration on one's breathing or repetition of a mantra) for the purpose of reaching a heightened level of spiritual awareness. Now before you think I am going all spiritual, or foo-foo, on you, please read this whole short section.

What if you could meditate in as short as 10 seconds per day?

What if this meditation could decrease stress levels, therefore decreasing your risks of disease, such as dry eyes, heart disease, neck pain, and more?

Meditation does NOT have to be an ultra spiritual, out-of-body experience only reserved for Buddhists in the mountains of Nepal. It can be, but it can also be highly beneficial for other reasons.

For this article, I am going to teach you how to do meditation to help decrease stress levels in as little as ten seconds.

How to Meditate to Decrease Disease Risk

This simple meditation technique can be used ANYWHERE. Whenever you're feeling stressed, depressed, anxious, nervous, or just need to get refocused. I use it several times a day when I am feeling flustered and need to get refocused or less stressed.

1. Close your eyes
2. Take a slow deep breath in. This deep breath in should take five seconds and you should count the five seconds in your head.
3. Hold your breath for two seconds
4. Then a long slow exhale for five seconds

INHALE FOR	1... 2... 3... 4...
HOLD BREATH FOR	5... 6...
EXHALE FOR	7... 8... 9... 10...

Click Here to watch the video for a simple meditation guide

Wrapping Up - YOU CAN DO THIS

I hope you enjoyed reading this book as much as I enjoyed writing it. We have seen drastic changes in our patients and customers around the world that have adopted this diet and healthy lifestyle. We often don't realize the fuel (food) that we are putting in our body is what is really the problem, because we are educated otherwise by the government, big business, and factory farms who have all the money.

Additionally, no doctor is going to heal you. We are trained in Western medicine which is mostly about symptom relief, not disease prevention. We (both Western trained doctors) believe in a different approach to medicine and it involves healing your body from the inside out with natural solutions, hydration, exercise, diet, and more. We did it and know you can do it too!

This will hopefully inspire you to take action and educate yourself even more! Please don't be afraid to reach out to myself or my wife in the Dry Eye Syndrome Support Community on Facebook to learn more, or visit our website, www. dryeyecommunity.com.

We Want To Hear About It

Nothing fulfills us more than seeing patients succeed with a plan that we have set out for them. Please share your successes with any of our programs or products on our facebook page and tag us if you can! Make sure to include pictures. Click here to head to our Facebook page (don't forget to like us).

Also if you know anyone that can benefit from our products or program, a referral is one of the biggest compliments you can give us! :)

Side Note on ALL Natural Treatments

EVERYONE SHOULD BE DOING THE FIRST LINE OF TREATMENT (Natural)... EVERYONE!!! Persevere with this first line of action items. It may take up to 6-8 weeks for the symptoms of dry eye to be managed. Some of these will have to be continued for life, but you will notice other ailments disappearing as you begin to implement these habits.

Useful links

- Click Here to Join the Dry Eye Syndrome Support Community on Facebook
- Follow Eye Love On
    - Facebook
    - YouTube
    - Twitter
    - Pinterest
    - Instagram
- www.dryeyecommunnity.com
- www.eyelovethesun.com

Join the Dry Eye Syndrome Support Community on Facebook

Use the code DRYEYE20 to get 20% off your first Heyedrate order on **Amazon**

Click here to shop: http://amzn.to/2xvBA7u

www.dryeyecommunity.com

Sources & Reference Materials

- Blind Faith by John Crittenden.
- The Kind Mama by Alicia Silverstone - We had the opportunity to meet Alicia in December 2016 and while we were already vegetarian, she completely shifted and rattled our beliefs even more. Her mission with her company, My Kind Organics, is incredible.
- Campbell and Campbell, China Study, 7, 89, 93, 184, 205, 230
- Gann et al., "Effects of a Low-Fat/High-Fiber Diet."
- Chavarro, Willett, and Skerrett, Fertility Diet, 44.
- "Position of the American Dietetic Association: Vegetarian Diets," Journal of the American Dietetic Association 109, no. 7 (July 2009); 1266-82
- "Doctors Endorse Vegan and Vegetarian Diets for Healthy Pregnancies," Physicians Committee for Responsible Medicine, http://www.pcrm.org/media/news/doctors-endorse-vegan-and-vegetarian-diets-for
- R. L. Blaylock, "A Possible Central Mechanism in Autism Spectrum Disorders, Part 3," Alternative Therapies In Health and Medicine 15, no. 2 (March-April 2009): 56-60, http://www.ncbi.nlm.nih.gov/pubmed/19284184 .
- "Organic Authority.com: 5 Food Labels That Mean Nothing," HuffPost Food, January 12, 2012, http://www.huffingtonpost.com/organic-authoritycom/5-food-labels-that-mean-n1/4b1/41202681.html
- Karl Weber, ed., Food, Inc. (New York: Public Affairs, 2009), 23. Robert W. Sears, MD, FAAP, and Amy Marlow, MPH, RD, CDN, HappyBaby: The Organic Guide to Baby's First 24 Months (New York: William Morrow Paperbacks, 2009), 24.
- M. Hansen et al., "Potential Public Health Impacts of the Use of Recombinant Bovine Somatotropin in Dairy Production," Prepared for a Scientific Review by the Joint Expert Committee on Food Additives, Consumers Union, September 1997, http://www.consumersunion.org/news/potential-public-health-impacts-of-the-use-of-recombinant-bovine-somatrotropin-in-dairy-production-part-1/.
- "Meat on Drugs," Consumer Reports, June 2012, https://www.consumersreports.org/content/dam/cro/news1/4articles/health/CR%20Meat%20On%20Drugs%20Report%2006-12.pdf

- R. Sears and Marlow, HappyBaby, 27. "Abuse of Antibiotics at Factory Farms Threatens the Effectiveness of Drugs Used to Treat Disease in Humans," Sierra Club, http://www.sierraclub.org/factoryfarms/factsheets/antibiotics.asp.

- "A Cesspool of Pollutants, Now Is the Time to Clean Up Your Body," McDougall Newsletter, August 17, 2004, https://www.nealhendrickson.com/PDF/PDFMc040800NL.pdf/

- "Dioxin & Furans: The Most Toxic Chemicals Known to Science, "Energy Justice Network, https://www.ejnet.org/dioxin.

- Arnold Schecter et al., "Intake of Dioxins and Related Compounds from Food in the US Population, "Journal of Toxicology and Environmental Health 63, no. 1 (May 11, 2001): 1-18, https://www.ejnet.org/dioxin/dioxininfood.pdf.

- Mark Hyman, MD, "Diary: 6 Reasons You Should Avoid It at All Costs Or Why Following the USDA Food Pyramid Guidelines is Bad for Your Health," Huffpost Healthy Living, http://www.huffingtonpost.com/ dr-mark-hyman/dairy-free-dairy-6-reasons1/4b1/4558876.html.

- Mark Bittman, "Got Milk? You Don't Need it," New York Times, July 7, 2012, http://opinionator.blogs.nytimes. com/2012/07/07/got-milk-you-dont- need-it/.

- "Lead Contamination of Chicken Eggs and Tissues from a Small Farm Flock," Journal of Veterinary Diagnostic Investigation 15, no. 5 (September 2003): 418-22, http://vdi.sagepub.com/ content/15/5/418.full.pdf.

- Hope Ferdowsian, MD, and Susan Levin, RD, "Fish Still Not a Healthy Choice," Providence Journal, October 24, 2006, http://www.pcrm.org/media/ commentary/fish-stil-not-a-healthy-choice.

- "Consumer Reports Investigation: Talking Turkey," Consumer Reports, http://www.consumerreports.org/turkey0613.

- "The Natural Human Diet," PETA, https://www.peta.org.living/vegatarian-living/the-natural-human-det.aspx.

- Neal Barnard, MD. "Meat Too Tough to eat," Heartford Courant, August 28, 2006, http://www.pcrm.org/media/ commentary/meat-too-tough-to-eat

- "Ask Dr. Sears: Artificial Sweeteners For Kids?," Parenting, http://www. parenting.com/article/ask-dr-sears- artificial-sweeteners-for-kids.

- "Trans Fats," American Heart Association, http://www.heart.org/ HEARTORG/GettingHealthy/ FatsAndOils/Fats101/Trans-4UCM1/43011201/4Article.jsp.

- "Trans Fat Is Double Trouble for Your Heart Health," Mayo Clinic, http:// www.mayoclinic.com/health/trans-fat/ CL00032.
- National Toxicology Program, CERHR Expert Panel Report for Bisphenol A, US Department of Health and Human Services, November 26, 2007. Breast Cancer Fund, Disrupted Development: The Dangers of Prenatal BPA Exposure, September 2013, http:// www.breastcancerfund.org/assets/pdfs/publications/disrupted-development-the-dangers-of-prenatal-bpa-exposure.pdf
- Disrupting Chemicals: From Basic Research To Clinical Practice (New York: Humana Press, 2007)

Medical Disclaimer

MEDICAL DISCLAIMER: THIS BOOK DOES NOT PROVIDE MEDICAL ADVICE

Eye Love LLC ("we" or "our"), a South Carolina Limited Liability Company, maintains this website for purposes of information, education, and communication. Nothing on this website should be construed as a promotion or solicitation for any products, or for the use of any product in a particular way that is not authorized by the laws and regulations of the country where the user is located.

The information, including but not limited to, text, graphics, images and other material contained on this website are for informational purposes only. The purpose of this website is to promote broad consumer understanding and knowledge of various health topics. It is not intended to be a substitute for professional medical advice, diagnosis or treatment.

Although practicing physicians, Doctors Travis and Jenna Zigler are not responsible for any actions taken by you, the consumer, after reading the information on this website. Always seek the advice of your physician or other qualified health care provider with any questions you may have regarding a medical condition or treatment and before undertaking a new health care regimen, and never disregard professional medical advice or delay in seeking it because of something you have read on this website.

We shall not be liable for any damage or injury that may arise from the use of or reliance upon any information provided on this website or from your inability to access the website. We assume no responsibility and shall not be liable for any damage or injury to you, your computer or other personal property including, but not limited to, damages caused by viruses that infect your computer equipment or other property on account of your access to our website or from your downloading of any materials, data, text, images, video or audio or other items from the website.

Eye Love, LLC, Dr. Travis Zigler, and/or Dr. Jenna Zigler do not recommend or endorse any specific tests, physicians, products, procedures, opinions or other information that may be mentioned on this website. Reliance on any information appearing on this website is solely at your own risk.

YOU FULLY AGREE AND UNDERSTAND THAT EYE LOVE, LLC IS NOT RESPONSIBLE FOR YOUR SUCCESS OR FAILURE AND MAKES NO REPRESENTATIONS OR WARRANTIES OF ANY KIND WHATSOEVER THAT OUR PRODUCTS OR SERVICES WILL PRODUCE ANY PARTICULAR RESULT FOR YOU.

AFFILIATE INFORMATION

Eye Love, LLC is a participant in the <u>Amazon Services LLC Associates Program</u>, an affiliate advertising program designed to provide a means for sites to earn advertising fees by advertising and linking to Amazon.com, Endless.com, MYHABIT.com, SmallParts.com, or AmazonWireless.com. Amazon, the Amazon logo, AmazonSupply, and the AmazonSupply logo are trademarks of Amazon.com, Inc. or its affiliates.

Just like if you purchase from us, if you click an affiliate link and purchase something from Amazon, you help with our mission to end preventable blindness!

Made in the USA
San Bernardino, CA
01 December 2017